First World War
and Army of Occupation
War Diary
France, Belgium and Germany

35 DIVISION
Divisional Troops
163 Brigade Royal Field Artillery
30 January 1916 - 8 September 1916

WO95/2475/1

The Naval & Military Press Ltd
www.nmarchive.com
Published in association with The National Archives

Published by

The Naval & Military Press Ltd

Unit 10 Ridgewood Industrial Park,

Uckfield, East Sussex,

TN22 5QE England

Tel: +44 (0) 1825 749494

www.naval-military-press.com

www.nmarchive.com

This diary has been reprinted in facsimile from the original. Any imperfections are inevitably reproduced and the quality may fall short of modern type and cartographic standards.

© **Crown Copyright**
Images reproduced by permission of The National Archives, London, England, 2015.

Contents

Document type	Place/Title	Date From	Date To
Heading	WO95/2475/1 35 Div Jan 16-Sept' 16 163 Brigade RFA		
Heading	35th Division 163rd Bde R.F.A. Jan-Sep 1916. Broken Up.		
Heading	War Diary 163rd Brigade RFA for period 1st to 8th September 1916. (Volume 8).		
War Diary	At Sea	30/01/1916	30/01/1916
War Diary	Havre	31/01/1916	01/02/1916
War Diary	Clety	02/02/1916	08/02/1916
War Diary	Marthes	09/02/1916	18/02/1916
War Diary	Bas Hamel	19/02/1916	29/02/1916
Heading	163 RFA Vol 2. 35 Div.		
War Diary	Bas Hamel	01/03/1916	08/03/1916
War Diary	Les Lauriers	09/03/1916	20/03/1916
War Diary	Bas Hamel	21/03/1916	26/03/1916
War Diary	Fleurbaix	27/03/1916	16/04/1916
War Diary	L'Epinette	17/04/1916	17/04/1916
War Diary	Paradis	18/04/1916	18/04/1916
War Diary	Paradis Nr Lestrem	19/04/1916	30/04/1916
Heading	D.A.G 3rd Echelon G.H.Q.	02/06/1916	02/06/1916
War Diary	Paradis Nr. Lestrem	01/05/1916	07/05/1916
War Diary	Paradis.	08/05/1916	13/05/1916
War Diary	Lacouture	14/05/1916	16/06/1916
War Diary	Cantrainne	17/06/1916	27/06/1916
War Diary	Monchy Breton	28/06/1916	30/06/1916
Miscellaneous	Medical & Sanitary Report of 163rd Bde R.F.A.	30/06/1916	30/06/1916
Heading	35th Division.163rd Brigade R.F.A. (West Ham) 1st to 31st July 1916		
Heading	War Diary of 163rd Brigade R.F.A. From 1st July, 1916 to 31st July 1916. Vol 6		
War Diary	Monchy Breton	01/07/1916	02/07/1916
War Diary	Authieule	03/07/1916	05/07/1916
War Diary	Gezaincourt	05/07/1916	06/07/1916
War Diary	Thievres.	06/07/1916	14/07/1916
War Diary	Varennes	14/07/1916	15/07/1916
War Diary	Bois Des Tailles	15/07/1916	20/07/1916
War Diary	Bronfay Farm.	20/07/1916	26/07/1916
War Diary	Near Maricourt	27/07/1916	31/07/1916
Miscellaneous	Summary of Medical and Sanitary Work for month ending July 31st 1916. Appendix I.	31/07/1916	31/07/1916
Miscellaneous	Expenditure of Communication Since Coming into Action as XIII Corps Area.		
Miscellaneous	Casualties Since date of Coming into action in XIII Corps area.	21/07/1916	21/07/1916
Heading	War Diary of 163rd (?) Brigade R.F.A.		
Miscellaneous	35th Divisional Artillery. 163rd Brigade Royal Field Artillery. August 1916		
Heading	War Diary of 163rd Brigade R.F.A. from August 1st-31st 1916 Volume 7		
War Diary	Near Maricourt	01/08/1916	01/08/1916

War Diary	Near Montauban	02/08/1916	12/08/1916
War Diary	Grovetown	13/08/1916	13/08/1916
War Diary	Bray	13/08/1916	13/08/1916
War Diary	Bois des Tailles North	14/08/1916	14/08/1916
War Diary	Ville-Sur-Ancre	15/08/1916	16/08/1916
War Diary	Maricourt.	16/08/1916	25/08/1916
War Diary	Bois Des Tailles North	26/08/1916	31/08/1916
Miscellaneous	D/1517 Sub Group	07/08/1916	07/08/1916
Miscellaneous	Ref attached Programme.	05/08/1916	05/08/1916
Operation(al) Order(s)	2nd Divisional Artillery Operation Order No. 27. Appendix I.	06/08/1916	06/08/1916
Operation(al) Order(s)	2nd Divisional Artillery Operation Order No. 29. Appendix II.	07/08/1916	07/08/1916
Operation(al) Order(s)	2nd Divisional Artillery Operation Order No. 30. Appendix III.	08/08/1916	08/08/1916
Miscellaneous	Medical & Sanitary Report of 163rd Bde R.F.A. for month ending 31st Aug 1916. Appendix IV.	31/08/1916	31/08/1916
War Diary	Bois Des Tailles	01/09/1916	02/09/1916
War Diary	Daours	03/09/1916	03/09/1916
War Diary	Molliens Au-Bois	04/09/1916	04/09/1916
War Diary	Monplaisir	05/09/1916	05/09/1916
War Diary	Mezerolles	06/09/1916	08/09/1916

WO 95/2475
35 Div.
Jan 16 – Sept 16
163 Brigade RFA

①

35TH DIVISION

163RD BDE R.F.A.
JAN - SEP 1916

Broken up

Army Form W. 3091.

Cover for Documents.

Nature of Enclosures.

SECRET

WAR DIARY.
163rd BRIGADE R.F.A.
for period
1st to 8th September 1916.
(Volume 8)

EnyS Moran Lt. Col.
Commanding 163rd Brigade R.F.A.

Notes, or Letters written.

WAR DIARY or INTELLIGENCE SUMMARY

Army Form C. 2118

(Erase heading not required.)

Place	Date	Hour	Summary of Events and Information	Remarks and references to Appendices
At Sea	30-1-16	11 P.M	Brigade left Burford via AMESBURY for SOUTHAMPTON en route for France. O.C. Lieut Col Guy Symonds. Adjutant Lt. C H Heath. Orderly Officer 2nd Lt Clarke Turvin. Medical Officer Lt. A S C Mackenzie RAMC. Vet Officer Lt. Cosgrove AVC. A. Battery Captain H L Syers Lt. W Hawrick 2nd Lts A. Todd and D. Hearn. B " " F C. Solomons 2nd Lts F S. King & A.C. Shakerley (G. Samuel sent to R.T.O). C " " D H.R. Richardson 2nd Lts D Hawrick, T. Green T L Cameron. D " Major Muirhead 2nd Lts D Munds Gibson D Abraham & A L Hearn. Bde A.C. Lieut Y goso 2nd Lts D Moore and C H Langtree. Seven hundred other ranks. Brigade sailed from SOUTHAMPTON at sun down on H.M.T.S's CAESERIA and NORTH WEST MILLER, latter ship also carrying Brigadier General Staveley C B. 35th Div Arty and staff.	Weather Fine but overcast Sea smooth
HAVRE	31-1-16	5 P.M	Brigade arrived HAVRE at day-break, disembarked 7 a.m, after endless and unnecessary delay A.B.C.& D batteries marched to No.2 rest camp. Bde Am Col to No.1 rest camp. Q.M.S. L. ENSELME, Chasseurs Alpin, French army joined as interpreter.	Weather Bright & cold, frost at night
"	1-2-16	11 P.M	H.Qs and "A" battery left HAVRE at 1.30 P.M. for ST OMER via ABBEVILLE "B" left at 5. P.M. "C" at midnight	Weather Bright all day, frost early morning and all night

WAR DIARY or INTELLIGENCE SUMMARY

Army Form C. 2118

(Erase heading not required.)

Place	Date	Hour	Summary of Events and Information	Remarks and references to Appendices
CLETY	2.2.16	10 P.M.	"A" battery and H.Q. arrived St OMER 6 a.m. marched to CLETY via WIZERNES arriving CLETY 1.P.M. "B" arrived CLETY 5 P.M. "C" battery who owing to a mistake probably on the part of R.T.O. ABBEVILLE left 3 officers and 60 men at that station arrived CLETY 11.P.M. "D" Battery left HAVRE 10 a.m. Am. Col. 6 a.m. Billets here ample and comfortable	Bright cold morning some rain later.
"	3.2.16	10.P.M.	Owing to non arrival of rations this day A B & C batteries had to eat part of iron ration. "D" battery arrived CLETY 11.45 a.m. Am Col 9 a.m.	Dull & cold morning showers later
"	4.2.16	8 P.M.	Cleaned up billets all day. C.R.A. visited billets first mail in and just out	Warm & raining all day
"	5.2.16	8.P.M.	General Pinney comdg 35th division inspected billets and remarked on good state of horses. C.R.A. passed mail inwards & outwards	Fine & cold all day
"	6.2.16	7.30 P.M	Voluntary church parade. O.C. took service, mail outwards	Rain early fine later
"	7.2.16	10 P.M	Brigade skeleton scheme neighbourhood of DOHEM and DELETTE. spoilt by heavy rain. Saw Mappin signaller in use by air line coy at DOHEM excellent. Preliminary orders received for move to AIRE district. small mail in mail out	Fine early heavy rain mid-day fine later.
"	8.2.16	8 P.M	Adjutant & interpreter went to reconnoitre new billets at MARTHES. Battery packing up. man of C. Batt badly kicked by a horse went to hospital at St OMER	Fine with some showers

1875 Wt. W593/826 1,000,000 4/15 J.B.C. & A. A.D.S.S./Forms/C. 2118.

WAR DIARY or INTELLIGENCE SUMMARY

Army Form C. 2118

(Erase heading not required.)

Place	Date	Hour	Summary of Events and Information	Remarks and references to Appendices
MARTHES	9.2.16	9.P.M.	Brigade moved off at 9 a.m. via THEROUANNE to MARTHES. Billeting receipts made out with Mayor, total claims 15 F settled. 5 Happer signallers received from Capt Yates R.E. DOHEM. 2nd Lt Samuel "B" Batty reported for duty. Brigade arrived MARTHES 11.50 A.M. Billets ample and comfortable. German bi-plane overhead all day. C.R.A. visited MARTHES	Cold and bright all day.
"	10.2.16	10 P.M.	Practical Happer signalling in morning. Large mail in and outwards. S.O. from Div H.Q (name unknown) visited camp. Order received for parade for to-morrow for inspection by Lord Kitchener.	Fine and cold all day. glass 10 P.M. 29.86
"	11.2.16	8 P.M.	Brigade paraded at 6 a.m. marched via CRECQUES and ROQUETOIRE to a point on road 1 mile N.E. of WITTES. There inspected by F.M. Lord Kitchener arrived home 1. P.M. march discipline fair but sense of direction poor in some batteries. Afternoon Adjutant to R.A. H.Q. O.C. to Div H.Q. for conference. Orders received for O.C. to attend senior officers course at AIRE	Heavy rain all day cold. Bar 8.P.M 29.4
"	12.2.16	8 P.M.	Horse lines in a bad state owing to rain, men employed clearing same. Afternoon lecture to men on grouping in XI corps 1st army. Evening officers conference on "notes on artillery". Mail inwards and out	Dull morning fine & bright later. Bar 7. P.M 30.275
"	13.2.16	7 P.M	CO went to course at AIRE. Church parade afternoon	Dull morning Bar 7 P.M. 30.1

WAR DIARY or INTELLIGENCE SUMMARY

Army Form C. 2118

(Erase heading not required.)

Instructions regarding War Diaries and Intelligence Summaries are contained in F. S. Regs., Part II. and the Staff Manual respectively. Title Pages will be prepared in manuscript.

Place	Date	Hour	Summary of Events and Information	Remarks and references to Appendices
MARTHES	14.2.16	8 P.M	C R A visited camp. Conference at R A H Q in afternoon Major Munshead attended in place of O.C. still on course at Aire	Rain early fine later Bar 8 P.M 30·1
"	15.2.16	8.P.M	C R A in camp. O C in AIRE, all officers not on duty attended a lecture by General HAKING in AIRE.	High wind all day. Bar 8 P.M 29·6
"	16.2.16	7.30 PM	Bad weather prevented C R A's inspection of our subsection for battery. Visual signalling lecture given to Signal Coy. O.C. still in AIRE	High wind & heavy rain Bar 8 P.M 29·6
"	17.2.16	8.P.M	Morning lecture and demonstration by Chemical adviser 1st army on use of gas helmets. 600 men attended. 2nd Lt Green gassed owing to improper fixing of helmet. Adjutant & interpreter to BAS HAMEL to reconnoitre billets. C O in AIRE	Fine all day Bar 8 P.M 29·8
"	18.2.16	8 P.M	C.O. returned at mid-day and went by motor to LOISNE N.E. of BETHUNE to see O.C. 120th Bde re attachment of men of 163 for instruction while former Bde now in the line. Lunched with C R A on way out. 2nd Lt. D Hearn "A" Battery to hospital suffering with bronchial asthma, pretty bad	Wet all day Fresh breeze in evening Bar 8 P.M. 29·75
BAS HAMEL	19.2.16	7. P.M	Brigade moved off at 9 P.M to BAS HAMEL via WITERNESSE and ISBERGUES. Delayed by 180th Bde (from home) moving into BLESSY. One man of D battery injured by horse falling on him. March discipline good specially B & D batteries. Arrived BAS. HAMEL 1 P.M. Good billets but Brigade very scattered. Lt Kilpatrick & 2nd Lt Hunter joined for duty. Mail out no mail in	Fine early cloudy later Bar 7 P.M. 30·15

WAR DIARY or INTELLIGENCE SUMMARY

Army Form C. 2118

(Erase heading not required.)

Place	Date	Hour	Summary of Events and Information	Remarks and references to Appendices
BASHAMEL	20-2-16	8 P.M	CRA and Bde Major visited camp saw Happen signalling. Batteries ran wire to Bde. H.Q. BCs meeting in evening. Lt Kilpatrick posted to B. battery 2nd Lt Hunter to A battery. Lt Goss started course in care of telephones	Fine and bright all day. Bar 8 P.M 30.4
" "	21-2-16	8 P.M	Lt Hanwick 2nd Lts Hanwick Shakely + Hearn and four men went to line as advance party. C.O. Capts Syres Richardson + Salmon. Lts Goss + Heath. 2nd/Lt Munro. Gibson + Langdon went to trench mortar school at ST VENANT. to see demonstration of Stokes trench mortar. Major Trunklead on a court martial. Lt Heath to MERVILLE for ammunition lecture. Sounds of very heavy firing to S.E. large mails out and in	Frosty morning fine all day. Bar 8 P.M 30.275
" "	22-2-16	8 P.M	2nd Lts Abraham, Green Todd + King and 116 men went to LOISNES to be attached to 170th Bde for three weeks. D.A.D.O.S 35th Div to lunch. Lt Heath took over duties of orderly officer 2nd Lt Clarke Turner took over duties of adjutant. Small mail inwards large mail out	Snow in morning froze in evening Bar 8 P.M 30.15
" "	23-2-16	8 P.M	Message from Lt. Hanwick saying that men on line had been ordered to eat their iron ration. A batty cart took up iron ration for A. B + D batteries. C. having taken theirs up. Doctor to ST VENANT. mail inwards and outwards	Some snow frying all day. Bar 8 P.M. 30.00

WAR DIARY or INTELLIGENCE SUMMARY

Army Form C. 2118

(Erase heading not required.)

Instructions regarding War Diaries and Intelligence Summaries are contained in F. S. Regs., Part II. and the Staff Manual respectively. Title Pages will be prepared in manuscript.

Place	Date	Hour	Summary of Events and Information	Remarks and references to Appendices
BAS HAMEL	24.2.16	8 P.M	Muirhead to aeroplane lecture. Sgns horse slipped on ice so could not go. C.O. to lunch at 158 and to ST VENANT. Sounds of heavy firing to S.E. Large mail out and in. Mail out but none in.	Hard frost all day. Bar 8 P.M. 29.92.
" "	25.2.16	8 P.M	C.O. with C.R.A to LOISNES saw 2nd Lts Shandy & Toad with part of A + B batteries in dry line, with 170th Bde. Very quick drive. Back by MERVILLE, saw artillery aeroven II corps General Carey, mail out. 70 bags mail in.	Hard frost all day snow in evening Bar 8 P.M. 30.25.
" "	26.2.16	8 P.M	Capt Sgns & C.O. to No 10 air squadron for lecture. Lt Heath left for line to be attached to 12D Bde for a week. B.C's to lia A.S.C. withdrawn all our waggons and promised to deliver rations to batteries of course they did not do so. rotten arrangement. Mail in and out.	Thaw set in about 10 a.m. Bar 8 P.M 29.6.
" "	27.2.16	8 P.M	C.O & Major Muirhead walked round N end of BOIS D'AUMONT. Chaplain held celebration at H.Q and church parades at battery billets. Evening C.O. went to 158 H.Q to meet C.R.A	Thaw all day. Bar 8 P.M. 29.5.
" "	28.2.16	8 P.M	C.O to ST VENANT Major Muirhead Capts Sgns & Richardson came to Bde H.Q in afternoon. Mail in and out.	Fine but cold all day Bar 8 P.M 29.55.
" "	29.2.16	8 PM	C.O. + Major Muirhead left for firing line at 9.30.a.m. Enemy aeroplane passed over camp about 10 a.m flying towards ISBERGUES, & returned shortly afterwards. Bomb dropped near and burst about ½ a mile from D Battery's billets.	Fine morning Rain afternoon & evening. Bar 8 PM. 29.3

1875 Wt. W593/826 1,000,000 4/15 J.B.C. & A. A.D.S.S./Forms/C. 2118.

G.M. Sigmondo Lt Col RFA

23 RTA 163
Vot 32
35?
fri

WAR DIARY
or
INTELLIGENCE SUMMARY
(Erase heading not required.)

Army Form C. 2118

Instructions regarding War Diaries and Intelligence Summaries are contained in F. S. Regs., Part II. and the Staff Manual respectively. Title Pages will be prepared in manuscript.

Place	Date	Hour	Summary of Events and Information	Remarks and references to Appendices
BAS HAMEL	1/3/16	8.P.M.	Whole Brigade had use of ST VENANT Baths from 8.30 am. till 12.30 pm. Lt. W.A. Hanwick returned from firing line. Regimental Sergeant-Major Smith left for the Base, having completed the 12 months extension of his engagement. Lt Hanwick returned from line. Mail in and out.	Fine all day. Bar. 8 P.M. 29.5.
"	2.3.16	8.P.M	C.O. and Major Muirhead returned from BETHUNE. Capts Szero and Richardson went to line for attachment to 122 Bde. R.F.A. Mail out, no mail in.	Fine morning, wet later. Bar 8 P.M 29.25
"	3.3.16	8.P.M.	C.R.A. and Bde Major came to Bde. H.Q., orders given to "D" batty to move up to line on 7th. 2nd Lt Hanwick returned from line. 2nd Lts Jackson & Garrett (T.C.) joined from Leyland, posted to Bde. Mail in and out.	Dull early, heavy rain in afternoon. Bar 8 P.M 29.45
"	4.3.16	8 P.M	Captain Richardson & Lt Heath returned from line, 2nd Lt Cannon went to line. 2nd Lt Jackson posted to D battery, 2/Lt Garrett posted to C Battery. O.C. went to D.A.C. St Venant and 158 H.Q. Zeppelin reported coming in this direction at 11 P.M. not seen by us. Mail in and out.	Snow & sleet all day. floods in places. Bar 8 P.M 29.5.
"	5.3.16 Sunday	8 P.M	Capt Stevens went to line, 2/Lt Shakerly returned. O.C. and Capt Richardson to La' LESTREM to see trench repair lights, did not take place owing to bad weather. German attacker dropped bomb 150 yds N.W. of Bde HQ hut. C.R.A. noted camp. Chaplain held service. Mail in and out.	Fine with some storm. Bar 8 P.M 29.95.

WAR DIARY or INTELLIGENCE SUMMARY

Army Form C. 2118

(Erase heading not required.)

Place	Date	Hour	Summary of Events and Information	Remarks and references to Appendices
BAS HAMEL	6.3.16	9 PM	C.O. to 157 HQ in morning. Message received that Gunner WOODLEY of C Batty attached to 122 on the line had been severely wounded by shrapnel. C.O. to see C.R.A. in evening. Mail out and in. New moon.	Snow in morning then and sunny later. Bar 9 PM 29.86
"	7.3.16	9 PM	Lt Heath and interpreter to Les LAURIERS to see new billets. 2nd Lt Moore to LESTREM and LEVANTIE on messages for C.O. 2nd Lt AL HEARN returned from line. Mail in and out.	Snow all day. Bar 9 PM 27.55
"	8.3.16	9 PM	Capt Stevens returned from the line. New R.S.M. joined. Orders received to move tomorrow to LES LAURIERS. C.R.A. came to H.Q. with C.O. who had been to meeting of Batt commanders at HAVERSKIRKE. 2nd Lt Hunter ordered back from the line having been guilty of unbecoming behaviour. Mail in and out.	Heavy snow early morning bright all day. Bar 9 PM 29.925
LES LAURIERS	9.3.16	9 PM	Battery moved off from BAS HAMEL at 8.45 a.m. to LES LAURIERS via ST VENANT and LE SART on the way passed 39th Division moving to ESTAIRES. Our waggons bombed at refilling point by german aeroplane. Billets good and comfortable, specially H.Q. in the chateau. Mail in and out.	Fine and frost all day. Bar 9 PM 29.25
"	10.3.16	8 PM	C.O. to see Col Wise commanding group 8th Division. Mail in and out.	Snow & sleet all day. Bar 9 PM 29.45
"	11.3.16	8 PM	C.O. to RAHQ. Lt Kilpatrick to hospital. Instructions received re C. Bty & ammn Col. Mail in & out.	Dull, some rain. Bar 29.65
"	12.3.16	8 PM	Capt ORMESBY JOHNSON representative from PM in chief called & gave various information re claims, paybooks &c. Voluntary Ch. parade at A Bty 6.30 p.m. Orders received re A Bty moving to line. Mail in & out.	Bar 29.55 8 pm
"	13.3.16	8 PM	O.C. A Bty reported to Col Wilson for instructions. O.O. rode to L.O at RAHQ & C, D Btys & A.C. Mail in & out.	Bar 29.66 8 pm

WAR DIARY or INTELLIGENCE SUMMARY

Army Form C. 2118

Instructions regarding War Diaries and Intelligence Summaries are contained in F. S. Regs., Part II. and the Staff Manual respectively. Title Pages will be prepared in manuscript.

(Erase heading not required.)

Place	Date	Hour	Summary of Events and Information	Remarks and references to Appendices
LES LAURIERS	14.3.16	8 P.M	A Battery went on to line attached to COL. WILSONS group 19th Division, position near CROIX BARBEE. Mail in and out. C.O. slept at R.A.H.Q.	Fine all day Bar 8 P.M 29.86
" "	15.3.16	9 P.M	C.O. returned from R.A.H.Q. in evening. O.O. to R.A.H.Q. re Divisional telephone lines. Mail out now in.	Fine all day Bar 8 P.M 29.74
" "	16.3.16	8 P.M	C.O. and O.O. to VIELLE CHAPELLE to see smoke bomb demonstration. 2nd Lt Samuel to line to be attached to 122 Bde. Mail in and out	Fine but colder Bar 8 P.M 29.7.0
" "	17.3.16	9 P.M	Lt Heath went to line, to erect telephone exchange. O.C. to MERVILLE. O.O. and Interpreter & Doctor to line. Mail in and out	Fine but dull all day Bar 9 P.M 29.97
" "	18.3.16	9 P.M	C.O. left for England on two days leave at midday. LT. KILPATRICK returned from hospital. D Battery relieved by C/122 at noon, & returned to wagon line. Mail in and out.	Fine slight rain in evening Bar 9 P.M 29.8
" "	19.3.16	9 P.M	Orders received for Bde H.Q., A & B Batteries to proceed to BAS HAMEL on 20th 21st. Mail in and out. Chaplain held services at B Battery's billets in morning.	Fine all day. Bar 9 P.M 29.7
" "	20.3.16	9.P.M.	Staff Captain visited Bde H.Q. in morning, in connection with move to BAS HAMEL. D Battery received orders to relieve C/122 during night of 20/21st; & to hand over 4 guns to C/122.	Fine. Bar 9 P.M. 29.6
BAS HAMEL	21.3.16	9 P.M	Bde H.Q., A & B Batteries returned to BAS HAMEL & reoccupied former billets. 1 Casualty reported among party under LT HEATH attached C/157	Dull with some rain Bar 9 P.M. 29.7

WAR DIARY or INTELLIGENCE SUMMARY

Army Form C. 2118

(Erase heading not required.)

Place	Date	Hour	Summary of Events and Information	Remarks and references to Appendices
BAS HAMEL	22.3.16	8 P.M	Mail in and out. CO on leave in England	Fine Bar 8 P.M 29.5
" "	23.3.16	8 P.M	CO returned from leave. Mr Enselin (interpreter) left on promotion. C battery an Am Coll returned from the line, mail in and out.	Fine day Bar 9 P.M 29.5
" "	24.3.16	8 P.M	Capts Syers, Richardson & Shuuns to line to choose positions. Mr Bonise joined as interpreter vice Enselin. Mail in and out	Snow early fine later Bar 8 P.M 29.5
" "	26.3.16	8 P.M	C. Battery left for line to relieve 8th Division. Lt Heath returned from line. CO to ST VENANT for lamb exhibition. C.R.A to billets saw ladder in use. Mail in and out	Snow early fine later Bar 8 P.M 29.7
" "	26.3.16	8.30 PM	Lt Heath went to line to arrange about billets for HQ, remainder of C & B batteries went to line. R.E O pip officer came to lunch, mail in and out	Cold but fine all day Bar 8 P.M 29.5
FLEURBAIX	27.3.16	8.30 PM	Bon HQ left BAS HAMEL at 11 a m and marched via ST VENANT MERVILLE and ESTAIRES to their billet, a poor billet. No mail in or out	Fine early wet later Bar 8 PM 29.47
"	28.3.16	8 P.M	CO visited A + C batteries, former at ROUE de QUESNE latter near ROUGE du BOUT. One man of A battery wounded by sniper. No mail in or out	Fine but cold high wind all day Bar 8 PM 29.2

WAR DIARY or INTELLIGENCE SUMMARY

(Erase heading not required.)

Army Form C. 2118

Place	Date	Hour	Summary of Events and Information	Remarks and references to Appendices
FLEURBAIX	29-3-16	8.30PM	CO to C battery and to RAHQ in evening, two small shell on wagon lines. Mail in and out	Fine but cold. Bar 8 PM 29.8
"	30-3-16	8 PM	CO to C battery who hit and fired farm house in German line, 2nd Lt FORSTER joined posted to Amn Coll. Mail in and out. Ady to A batt. DO to DB+A.	Very fine weather. Bar 8 PM 30.425
"	31-3-16	8.P.M	2/Lt Forster joined from England and posted to the Amn Col. Major Muirhead + Lt Goss came to HQ. Mail in and out.	Very fine and warmer. Bar 8 PM 30.40
"	1-4-16	8 PM	~~CO to lunch at Div HQ Lt Laidlaw + 2nd Lt Daly to tea mail in and out~~	Very fine and warmer.

Guy Symons Lt Col.
com ag (6 3 19 (How) Bde R.F.A.

WAR DIARY or INTELLIGENCE SUMMARY

(Erase heading not required.)

Army Form C. 2118

163 RFA Vol 3

Place	Date	Hour	Summary of Events and Information	Remarks and references to Appendices
FLEURBAIX	1-4-16	8 PM	CO to Div HQ to lunch. to LEVANTI to sketch. Lt Laidlaw and 2nd Lt Darby + chaplain to Div. Mail in and out.	Fine and warm Bar 8 PM 30.2
"	2-4-16	9.30 PM	O.C to left group H.Q. there met General Carey + C.R.A round front with C.R.A to choose forward How positions. Capt Simons + Lt Ross to Bde H.Q. Sketch board finished and tried successfully. O.C to C.R.E saw dum taken for How mounting. Wh + Own right group carried out bombardment at night. Mail in and out.	Fine and very warm. Bar 9.30 PM 30.10
"	3-4-16	8.30	Lt YOULL from D.AC joined posted to B battery. C.O round O.P's before breakfast mail in and out.	Fine + warm Bar 8.30 PM 30.1
"	4-4-16	9 PM	CO inspected wagon line under A.D.V.S afternoon chose battery position incl O.C. D batty. C.R.A to H.Q in evening, inspected new sketch board mail in and out	Fine and warm Bar 8 PM 30.00
"	5-4-16	8 PM	C.O to C.R.E in afternoon Col Bradford and Fawcett and Major Parson to Bde H.Q. CO to A battery mail in and out.	Fine Bar 8PM 29.95
"	6-4-16	8 PM	CO and O.C met C.R.A and C.R.E at R.E.W.S, then to choose position for How in Right action. Capt Coxall visited Bde H.Q. Mail in and out.	Fine but cold Bar 8 PM 29.90
"	7-4-16	8 PM	O.C round O.P's with C.R.A. C.R.A to Bde HQ in evening. OC and party from HQ staff worked on the HOLE OP till midnight mail in and out	Wet early fine later Bar 8 PM 30.000
"	8-4-16	8 PM	CO to haystack position. Orderly Officer to BAC ST. MAUR. R.A divisional Workshop started this day. FLEURBAIX shelled by S.9 at 5 PM. O.P progress report sent in mail in and out	Fine + bright all day. Bar 8 PM 30.10

1875. Wt. W593/826 1,000,000 4/15 J.B.C. & A. A.D.S.S./Forms/C. 2118.

WAR DIARY or INTELLIGENCE SUMMARY

Army Form C. 2118

(Erase heading not required.)

Place	Date	Hour	Summary of Events and Information	Remarks and references to Appendices
FLEURBAIX	9-4-16	8 P.M.	CO with CRA to LEVANTIE and round gun positions, evening CO to OP line. Mail in and out. Major Muirhead O.C. D. Battery to course at AIRE	Fine and bright Bar 8PM 30.15
" "	10-4-16	8.30 PM	CO on OP line all day. Mr Dukes signalling officer 19th Div RA visited HQ. CO and OO out on night working party job. Regt group have chaffs. Mail in and out	Fine and warm all day Bar 8PM 29.75
" "	11-4-16	8.30 PM	CO to A battery before breakfast, to workshop of in morning. Lt Young of 2nd corps artillery to see switchboard. CO to RAHQ in evening. Xmas present to driver. Mail in and out.	Wet all day Bar 8.30PM 29.80
" "	12-4-16	8.30 PM	CO to RA house met General Carey. CO and OO to BAILLEUL to see switch board, then to 21st Siege battery. Mail in and out.	Wet all day Bar 8 PM 29.55
" "	13-4-16	8 PM	CRA visited Bde HQ. CO and OO to Workshop. Lt Goss to lunch. 2/Lt Moore returned from trench mortar course. Mail out none in.	Fine with high wind Bar 8PM 29.50
" "	14-4-16	8.30 PM	CO to R.A.HQ. O.O. to take over exchange on new sector day on winding scheme. Major Wood R.E. topographical section to Bde H.Q. mail in and out	Wet & cold Bar 8.30PM 29.65
" "	15-4-16	9.30 PM	O.O. to new billet area. CO to OP.F. line. C.R.A. visited Bde H.Q. Lt P.J. Turner A.V.C. joined Bde. Mail in and out	Fine and cold Bar 9.30PM 30.10
" "	16-4-16	9. P.M.	Carried out experiments firing How at high elevations. C.R.A. present. Mail in and out. D batty & B.A.C. left for new billet.	Fine all day Bar 9 P.M. 30.00
L'EPINETTE	17-4-16	9 P.M.	Bde HQ & A Battery moved to new billets. Billets allotted to Bde H.Q. at PARADIS found to be occupied by 10th Welsh Regt. Other quarters found for night at L'EPINETTE. CO remained at SAILLY with CRA of 1st Australian Division. Mail in & out	Rain & wind all day. Bar 29.6 9.PM
PARADIS	18-4-16	9 PM	Bde H.Q. moved to billets allotted at PARADIS. CO still at SAILLY. Mail in & out.	Rain & wind all day. Bar 9.PM 29.2

ement
WAR DIARY or INTELLIGENCE SUMMARY

(Erase heading not required.)

Army Form C. 2118

Instructions regarding War Diaries and Intelligence Summaries are contained in F. S. Regs., Part II. and the Staff Manual respectively. Title Pages will be prepared in manuscript.

Place	Date	Hour	Summary of Events and Information	Remarks and references to Appendices
PARADIS Nr LESTREM	19-4-16	9 P.M	O.C at SAILLY. 2nd Lt. D. Hearn rejoined from hospital, mail in and out, at Bde H.Q. A & B batteries and B.A.C. C & D batteries in the line	Wet & cold Bar 8 PM 29.5
"	20.4.16	8 P.M.	C.O returned from SAILLY. German aeroplane passed over at 2 P.M. Chaplain visited Bde H.Q. mail in and out	Fine but cold Bar 8 PM 29.4.85
"	21.4.16	8 P.M	C.O to R.A workshop there met General Carey comdg R.A XI corps. Later C.O to O.P line mail in and out. Capt Shaw transferred to B.A.C. Lt Goss to B Batty	Fine but sunny Bar 29.45
"	22.4.16	9 P.M.	Major Murdoch Corps signals came to see switch board. C.O & O.O to C Batty O.C to R.A H.Q in evening mail in and out	Wet all day Bar 9 P.M. 29.7.
"	23.4.16	8.30 PM	O.C to R.A.H.Q. and with General to D A's battery position, afterwards up in observation balloon, afterwards to conference at R.A.H.Q. Interpreter went to column mail in and out	Fine & clear all day Bar 8.30 PM 30.2
"	24.4.16	8.30 P.M	C.O to R.A H.Q and later round O.P line. School of instruction started at 157 H.Q. mail in and out	Fine all day Bar 8.30 PM 30.22
"	25.4.16	8 P.M	C.O, O.O and Lt Goss to workshop. Cols Nasha & Bellairs visited Bde HQ in the afternoon. 2/Lt Shakerly returned to B Co. 2/Lt Hender from A to D on loan mail in and out	Fine all day Bar 8 P.M. 30.26
"	26.4.16	8 P.M	C.O at workshop all day. C.R.A came to dinner at Bde H.Q mail in and out	Fine all day Bar 8 PM 30.1
"	27.4.16	9 P.M	C.O to O.Ps of night group and to C battery line O.P for strafe. C.R.A. to Bde H.Q.	Fine & warm Bar 8 PM 30.1
"	28.4.16	9 P.M	C.O round horse lines with A.D.V.S. O.O to BETHUNE for orders. Capt Syers & Lt Goss to Bde H.Q in afternoon. mail in and out. GAS and B.M COL Billets turned out	Fine & warm Bar 8.30 PM 30.1
"	29.4.16	9 P.M	O.O to BETHUNE. Adj to R.A H.Q. Engines on fire at our Coll billet. C.R.A visited H.Q. mail in and out.	Fine with high wind Bar 9 PM 30.05

WAR DIARY
or
INTELLIGENCE SUMMARY
(Erase heading not required.)

Army Form C. 2118

Instructions regarding War Diaries and Intelligence Summaries are contained in F. S. Regs., Part II. and the Staff Manual respectively. Title Pages will be prepared in manuscript.

Place	Date	Hour	Summary of Events and Information	Remarks and references to Appendices
Paradis near Lestrem	30/4/16	9 P.M.	C.O. & O.O. left for D Battery position	Fine & warm Bar. 9 pm 30.05
			R C Turner Lieut & Adjt for Commdg. 163 F.A. Bde.	

DAG,
3rd Echelon, GHQ.

Herewith War Diary
for the month of May.

2/6/16

Resume th.
as/Adjt 163 FA Bde

[stamp: 163rd BRIGADE ROYAL FIELD ARTILLERY]

WAR DIARY or INTELLIGENCE SUMMARY

(Erase heading not required.)

Army Form C. 2118

163 RFA
Vol 4

Place	Date	Hour	Summary of Events and Information	Remarks and references to Appendices
PARADIS to LESTREM	1/5/16	9.PM	C.O. & O.O. at D Battery position. Order received from 35. Div. Arty that Lt Col Symonds is to take command of RIGHT GROUP 35 D.A. from 6 P.M. 3rd inst. Mail in & out	Fine & warm Bar 9 PM 29.95
"	2/5/16	9 PM	C.O. & O.O at D Battery position. Mail in and out	Fine & warm slight showers Bar 9 PM 29.9
"	3/5/16	9.PM	D.D.V.S. inspected horses of all Batteries except D, & found their condition satisfactory. C.O. & O.O moved to Right Group Headquarters in afternoon. C.O. took over command at 6 pm. Mail in and out.	Fine & warm Bar 9 PM 29.82
"	4/5/16	9 PM	D.D.V.S. visited D Battery wagon line. Mail in and out.	Fine. Bar 9 PM 29.6
"	5/5/16	9 PM	Board of enquiry held to assess damage caused by fire at Ammn Col. Billet. Mail in and out.	Fine & warm slight showers Bar 9 PM 29.4
"	6/5/16	9 PM	Capt. Russell RFA posted to Brigade took over command of D Battery at 6 a.m.	Fine. Some showers. Bar 9 PM 29.6
"	7/5/16	9 PM	Posting of Capt. Russell cancelled. Returned to 19th Div. C.O. visited Bde H.Q. Lt Heath moved from Right Group H.Q. to C/163 Battery position. Mail in and out	Cool & showers Bar 9 PM 29.65

WAR DIARY or INTELLIGENCE SUMMARY

Army Form C. 2118

Instructions regarding War Diaries and Intelligence Summaries are contained in F. S. Regs., Part II. and the Staff Manual respectively. Title Pages will be prepared in manuscript.

(Erase heading not required.)

Place	Date	Hour	Summary of Events and Information	Remarks and references to Appendices
PARADIS	8/5/16	9 P.M.	Mail in + out. Nothing to record	Cooler and Showery. Bar 9PM 29.8
"	9/5/16	9 PM	Nothing to record	Cool + showery Bar 9PM 29.8
"	10/5/16	9 PM	" "	Fine Bar 9 PM 30.1
"	11/5/16	9 PM	" "	Fine Bar 9PM 30.2
"	12/5/16	9 PM	Adjutant visited Right Group H.Q. to see C.O. regarding move of Bde H.Q. to Lacouture. Mail in + out.	Fine Bar. 9PM 29.95
"	13/5/16	9 PM	2/Lt Maitland-Heriot joined Bde. Posted to D Battery; temporarily attached to B.A.C. D Battery left for Molinghem for a course of Training under O.C. 121st. Bde. R.F.A. Mail in + out.	Warm. Bar 9PM 29.90 Showery+cool.
LACOUTURE	14/5/16	9 PM	Bde H.Q. moved to Lacouture, occupying former H.Q. of Right Group. Lt. Col Bedford commanding 159 Bde R.F.A. temporarily joins H.Q. mess. Lt. Col. Symonds still in command of Right Group + living at Right Group new H.Q. Lt Heath still at C. Battery position	Fine cool. Bar 9PM. 30.00
"	15/5/16	9 PM	Nothing of importance to record.	Fine Bar 9.PM 30.1

WAR DIARY or INTELLIGENCE SUMMARY

Army Form C. 2118

(Erase heading not required.)

Place	Date	Hour	Summary of Events and Information	Remarks and references to Appendices
LACOUTURE	16.5.16	8 P.M.	Lt. Col. Symonds & Capt. Richardson dined at Bde H.Q. Orders received regarding reorganisation of Divisional Artillery. 163 Bde to take one battery from each 18pdr Bde & to lose A, B, & C Batteries. Half B.A.C. to go to D.A.C. Remainder to Base.	Very fine. Bar. 30.2
"	17.5.16	9 P.M.	Capt Stevens goes on leave.	Fine Bar 30.2 9 P.M
"	18.5.16	9 P.M.	Lt.Col Symonds, Capt Richardson, & Lt Heath at Bde H.Q. to confer re clearing up Bde accounts. Lt. Col. Bedford leaves Bde H.Q. for Base.	Fine Bar 9 P.M. 30.4
"	19.5.16	9 P.M.	Brig General Staveley & Lt.Col Symonds at Bde H.Q. in the evening.	Fine. Bar 9 P.M 30.42
"	20.5.16	9. P.M.	Nothing to record.	Fine. Bar 9 P.M 30.5
"	21.5.16	9 P.M.	Adjt. visited Trenches with Lt Col Symonds. In the afternoon saw Lt Col Besly regarding reorganisation of Column & evacuation of surplus personnel.	Fine. Bar 9 P.M 30.5
"	22.5.16	9 P.M.	Captain H.C. Staveley, Chaplain, joined Bde H.P. D/163 returned from Course of training. 2/Lt Forster joined B Battery.	Fine Some Showers Bar 9 P.M. 30.4
"	23.5.16	9 P.M.	2/Lt L.A. Heawn at Bde H.Q. 2/Lt Maitland Heriot joins D Battery.	Fine Bar 9 P.M. 30.2
"	24.5.16	9 P.M.	Nothing to record	Some rain Bar 9 P.M 30.0

WAR DIARY or INTELLIGENCE SUMMARY

Army Form C. 2118

Instructions regarding War Diaries and Intelligence Summaries are contained in F. S. Regs., Part II. and the Staff Manual respectively. Title Pages will be prepared in manuscript.

(Erase heading not required.)

Place	Date	Hour	Summary of Events and Information	Remarks and references to Appendices
Inconiture	25.5.16	8 PM	Amm. Col. comes under command of Lt. Col. Berly, commdg 35th DAC	Some showers mostly fine Bar. 8 PM 29.8
"	26.5.16	9 PM	Lt. Col. Symonds hands command of Right Group to O.C. 157 Bde & returns to Bde H.Q. Left for England on leave in the evening	Fine. Cooler Bar 9 PM 29.8
"	27.5.16	9 PM	Nothing to record.	Fine. Bar 9 PM 29.9
"	28.5.16	9 PM	Reorganization of Brigade takes effect from midnight 27/28. A Battery transferred to 157 Bde, B Bty to 158, C Bty to 159. D/157 D/158 D/159 transferred to 163. New A Battery in action in Right Group, B Battery in action in Left Group. One section C Battery in action Right Group, one section in Left Group. Major Parsons commdg A Battery at R.A. H.Q. acting Bde Major in absence of Major Robinson. Capt Keith commands battery temporarily, being lent by DAC. Capt Crocker, commdg B Battery absent on leave. Lt Worsley in charge. Capt Sanderson in command of C Battery. Adjutant visits A Battery.	Fine. Bar 9 PM 29.9
	29.5.16	9 PM	Adjutant visits B Battery. Section of C Battery in action in Left Group. Orders received for D Battery to go into action to relieve D/159.	Fine Slight rain in evening Bar 9 PM 30.0
	30.5.16	9 PM	Adjutant visits C Battery.	Rain in morning Fine later Bar 9 PM 30.1
	31.5.16	9 PM		

WAR DIARY
or
INTELLIGENCE SUMMARY
(Erase heading not required.)

Army Form C. 2118

Instructions regarding War Diaries and Intelligence Summaries are contained in F. S. Regs., Part II. and the Staff Manual respectively. Title Pages will be prepared in manuscript.

Place	Date	Hour	Summary of Events and Information	Remarks and references to Appendices
LACOUTURE	31.5.16	9 P.M.	Capt. Crocker, B Battery, returns from leave.	Fine. Bar. 9pm 30.1

R.C. Turner Lt. & Adjt.
for Lieut. Col. R.F.A.
Commanding 168rd Bde R.F.A.

WAR DIARY or INTELLIGENCE SUMMARY

~~XXXV~~ 165 Bde R.F.A. Vol 5

Army Form C. 2118

Place	Date	Hour	Summary of Events and Information	Remarks and references to Appendices
LACOUTURE	1/6/16	9PM	Lt Heath returns to Bde H.Q. D Battery comes into action in position vacated by D/159	Bar 9PM 30.05
"	2/6/16	9PM	Lt Goss D/159 temporarily takes command of D/163	Fine Bar. 9PM 30.1
"	3/6/16	9PM	Lt Heath reconnoitres routes for proposed O.P. wires in connection with R.A. Divisional Scheme. Brig. General Stavely, visits R.A. workshop in morning.	Fine Bar. 9PM 30.05
"	4.6.16	9PM	Lt Heath working on O.P. wires as above.	Fine. Bar 9PM. 29.7
"	5.6.16	9PM	Lt Heath working on O.P. work as above.	Some rain in morning. Fine later. Bar. 9PM 29.55
"	6/6/16	9PM	Lt Heath preparing routes for buried wire to O.P.s	Rain. Fine in evening. Bar 9PM 29.75
"	7/6/16	9PM	C.O. returns from leave.	Fine. Bar 9PM 29.7
"	8/6/16	9PM	C.O. attends conference at R.A. Headquarters.	Showery Bar 9PM. 29.8
"	9.6.16	9PM	C.O. attends conference at Left group H.Q.	Showery Bar. 9PM 29.9

WAR DIARY or INTELLIGENCE SUMMARY

Army Form C. 2118

(Erase heading not required.)

Place	Date	Hour	Summary of Events and Information	Remarks and references to Appendices
LACOUTURE	10.6.16	9 P.M.	Orders received for B Battery to move to area of 61st Div. Arty. C.O. placed in charge of Divisional Scheme for digging cable trench.	Showery Bar. 9 P.M. 30.1.
"	11.6.16	9 P.M.	C.O. visits O.Ps with General Stanely. Later arranges for collecting of Cable Trench Party (250 men) at Richebourg.	Showery Bar. 9 P.M. 30.2.
"	12.6.16	10 P.M.	C.O. & Lt. Heath supervising digging of cable trench.	Wet. Bar 9 P.M. 29.9
"	13.6.16	9 P.M.	B Battery moves to 61st Divisional area. 2/Lt. Taggart, A Battery, goes on R.H.A. Course. Notice of probable move received.	Wet Bar. 9 P.M. 29.8
"	14.6.16	9 P.M.	Lt. Col. Allardyce of 39th Div. visits Bde H.Q. in connection with taking over of Bde H.Q.	Wet. Bar. 9 P.M. 30.125
"	15/6/16	9 P.M.	C.O. supervising digging of cable trench. Visits 28th Heavy Group H.Q. in afternoon.	Wet Bar 9 P.M. 30.0
"	16.6.16	9 P.M.	Lt. Col. Taylor, comdg 28th Heavy Group visits Bde H.Q. Orders received regarding move of Brigade into Divisional Rest.	Fine warmer Bar. 9 P.M. 30.05

WAR DIARY or INTELLIGENCE SUMMARY

(Erase heading not required.)

Army Form C. 2118.

Place	Date	Hour	Summary of Events and Information	Remarks and references to Appendices
CANTRAINNE	17.6.16	8 P.M.	Bde H.Q. 1 Section of C/163 & 1 Section of D/163 moves to Cantraine	Bar 8 P.M. 50-126
"	18.6.16	9 P.M.	Remainder "C" Battery moves to Cantraine	Bar 9 P.M. 30-1
"	19.6.16	10 P.M.	Remainder "D" Battery moves to Cantraine. B Battery still under 61st Div Arty with 39th Div. C.O. visits R.A.H.Q. Major Parsons rejoins "A" Battery	Bar 10 P.M. 30-1
"	20.6.16	10 P.M.	B Battery moves to Cantraine from the line	Bar 10 P.M. 30-2
"	21.6.16	9 P.M.	Conference of Battery Commanders at Bde H.Q. in evening	Bar 9 P.M. 30-2
"	22.6.16	9 P.M.	Brigade takes part in Divisional Artillery Route March. C.O. at R.A.H.Q. in evening	Bar 9 P.M. 30-1
"	23.6.16	9 P.M.	Nothing to record	Bar 9 P.M. 30-20 Heavy rain in afternoon
"	24.6.16	9 P.M.	All Officers of Brigade take part in tactical exercise under C.R.A.	Bar 9 P.M. 30-1

WAR DIARY or INTELLIGENCE SUMMARY

Army Form C. 2118.

(Erase heading not required.)

Instructions regarding War Diaries and Intelligence Summaries are contained in F. S. Regs., Part II. and the Staff Manual respectively. Title Pages will be prepared in manuscript.

Place	Date	Hour	Summary of Events and Information	Remarks and references to Appendices
Cantraine	26/6/16	9 p.m.	C.O. to Doshens re "flappers" for signalling.	Fine Bar 9 p.m. 30.075
"	27/6/16	9 p.m.	Rev. Staveley leaves for England. C.O. at Merville + Div. Sub-park.	Wet Bar 9 p.m. 29.8
MONCHY-BRETON	28/6/16	9 p.m.	Orders received for Bde (less A Battery) to move to Monchy Breton. Bde H.Q. moves at 4 p.m. Batteries at 9 p.m.	
"	29/6/16		Battery commanders to Arras to reconnoitre positions in the event of Bde moving to 5th Div Area.	
"	30/6/16		Lt March + 2/Lt Meade Jetson to Arras.	

Appendix. Summary of medical & sanitary work.

R E Turner Lt.
a/A. 163 F.A. Bde

Medical + Sanitary Report.   2465 2nd Bn. R.W.F.
                                     for month ending June 30.

1. **Medical.**
   (a) Summary: General health good. Troops - past fortnight rather slight - outbreaks, colds, rheumatism. Dental accidents, chiefly from damp, te, te. All these cases were treated with unit.

   (b) In Hospital - on case I Pyrexia Unknown
                    "   "   I Slight Shrapnel Wd.
                    "   "   Injury from gunwire
                    "   "   Bronchitis
                    "   "   Septic abscess (neck)
                    "   "   Severe kick (R-leg)

   (c) No Infectious Diseases.

2. **Sanitation.**
   (a) Water - supplies good - + efficiently chlorinated
   (b) Latrines - apt to get foul type in general use
   (c) Cook-houses, kitchens, stoves te. in good condition - utilised use of chloride of lime.
   (d) Dry-fry receptacle orderly possible.
   (e) Horse-manure burnt in incinerators or carted away by farmers.

                                     (sgd). Aldridge Hugh
                                           Capt. R.A.M.C.

WAR DIARY

163rd BRIGADE R. F. A. (West Ham)

1st to 31st JULY 1916.

35th Division.

Vol 6

Cover for Documents.

Nature of Enclosures.

Confidential
War Diary
of
163rd Brigade R.F.A.

From 1st July 1916 to 31st July 1916.

Munro Lt Col
Comdg 163rd Bde R.F.A

WAR DIARY
or
INTELLIGENCE SUMMARY

(Erase heading not required.)

Army Form C. 2118.

Place	Date	Hour	Summary of Events and Information	Remarks and references to Appendices
MONCHY BRETON	1.7.16		C.O. and ADJT visit 15th Bde, 5th Div. at ARRAS to reconnoitre billets and positions. 2/Lt MORGAN to ARRAS. A Battery rejoins the Bde from RICHEBOURG.	Ref
"	2.7.16		Bde receives orders to move to AUTHIEULE near DOULLENS & marches at 1. A.M. night of 2nd/3rd. 2/LT. MENDS-GIBSON & LT MARCH rejoin Bde from ARRAS	Ref
AUTHIEULE	3.7.16	10.30 AM	Bde arrives AUTHIEULE.	Ref
"	4.7.16	-	Bde remains at AUTHIEULE.	Ref
"	5.7.16	11.15 am	Bde moves to GEZAINCOURT	
GEZAINCOURT	"	4 pm	Orders received that Bde is to proceed on the 6th to THIEVRES	Ref
"	6.7.16	11.45 am	Bde moves off.	
THIEVRES	"	3 pm	Bde arrives THIEVRES.	Ref
	7.7.16		2/Lt REID joins Brigade from DAC	Ref

WAR DIARY
or
INTELLIGENCE SUMMARY

(Erase heading not required.)

Army Form C. 2118.

Place	Date	Hour	Summary of Events and Information	Remarks and references to Appendices
THIEVRES	8.7.16		C.O. visits G.H.Q. information bureau, BEAUQUESNE in the morning. Reconnaissance of routes to proposed positions by all available officers in the afternoon.	Ref
	9.7.16		C.O. visits ALBERT with G.O.C.R.A. & O.C. 159 Bde R.F.A.	Ref
	10.7.16		G.O.C.R.A. inspects Z 35 T.M. Battery. C.O. present.	Ref
	11.7.16		Nothing to record.	Ref
	12.7.16	12 noon	Battery commanders proceed to 12th Div. H.Q. to reconnoitre positions	
		2.30pm	Orders received to stand by in readiness to move.	
		5pm	B.C.s return, orders re reconnaissance of positions having been cancelled.	
	13.7.16	10.30am	C.O. with other Bde commanders proceed to reconnoitre another area	Ref
		3pm	Orders received to move to VARENNES-HARPONVILLE-WARLOY area on 14th	Ref

WAR DIARY or INTELLIGENCE SUMMARY

Army Form C. 2118.

Place	Date	Hour	Summary of Events and Information	Remarks and references to Appendices
THIEVRES	14.7.16	8.30 a.m.	Bde moves off, marching via MARIEUX & PUCHEVILLERS	
VARENNES	—	2 pm	Bde arrives VARENNES.	
"		9 pm	Orders received for Bde to move on 15th to BOIS DES TAILLES, via BRAY	Ret
"	15.7.16	5.40 a.m.	Bde moves off, marching via HENNENCOURT, LAVIEVILLE, BUIRE.	
BOIS DES TAILLES.	"	11.30 a.m.	BOIS DES TAILLES reached.	Ret
	16.7.16	5 pm	G.O.C. & C.R.A. visit camp.	Ret
	17.7.16	—	C.O. & battery commanders visit the line	Ret
	18.7.16	—	O.O. & seconds in command visit the line.	Ret
	19.7.16	—	Adjt. & other officers visit the line. Bde moves from South camp to North camp of BOIS DES TAILLES	
	"	11.30 p.m.	B.C.s to line with detachments of 1 section per battery to take over from 148 Bde, 30th Div.	Ret
	20.7.16	7.30 a.m.	C.O. & O.O. leave for line.	Ret
	"	9.30 a.m.	Remainder of Bde, under Adjutant, leaves for line.	Ret

WAR DIARY or INTELLIGENCE SUMMARY

Army Form C. 2118.

Instructions regarding War Diaries and Intelligence Summaries are contained in F. S. Regs., Part II. and the Staff Manual respectively. Title Pages will be prepared in manuscript.

(Erase heading not required.)

Place	Date	Hour	Summary of Events and Information	Remarks and references to Appendices
BRONFAY FARM	20.7.16	12.30pm	Bde take up wagon lines & Bde H.Q. near BRONFAY FARM, between BILLON WOODS and CEYLON WOODS	
		10pm	B.C.s take over command of batteries they are relieving (30th Division) D Battery comes under command of MAJ. KIRKLAND, OC 'A' GROUP. Remaining batteries under LT.COL. STEWART, OC 'D' GROUP.	
	21.7.16	10am	Bde H.Q. & wagon lines move to new camp near GREAT BEAR COPSE.	Act
	22.7.16	—	C.O. moves to R.A. H.Q.	Act
	22.7.16	8pm	C.O. Adjt + O.O. laying wire from MACHINE GUN COPSE to HARDECOURT for C.R.A. One telephonist wounded during this.	Act
	23.7.16	7am	Laying of wire completed.	Act
		9am	Wire laid for C.R.A. from MARICOURT to R.A.H.Q. by O.O.	Act
	24.7.16	—	Nothing to record.	Act
	25.7.16	—	C.O. returns to Bde H.Q.	Act

WAR DIARY or INTELLIGENCE SUMMARY

Army Form C. 2118.

(Erase heading not required.)

Place	Date	Hour	Summary of Events and Information	Remarks and references to Appendices
BRONFAY FARM	26.7.16	4 pm	C.O. leaves Camp to take over command of C Sub Group. H.Q. near MARICOURT	X-countersigs A/151 B/151 C/151 D/150 (all 30th Div)
near MARICOURT	27.7.16	5 am	Adjutant and O.O. join C.O. with Bde Staff.	
		7.10 am	Sub-group supported our infantry in attack on LONGUEVAL & DELVILLE WOOD. Attack unsuccessful.	
		12.45 pm to about 6 pm	Counter attack repulsed by infantry, supported by artillery.	
	28.7.16	—	18 pdr. batteries of Group firing on wire in neighbourhood of GUILLEMONT & FALFEMONT all day. Howitzers on line of Trees S.W. of GUILLEMONT.	
		11.30 pm to 1.30 am	All batteries cease firing: patrols out.	

WAR DIARY or INTELLIGENCE SUMMARY

Army Form C. 2118.

(Erase heading not required.)

Place	Date	Hour	Summary of Events and Information	Remarks and references to Appendices
NEAR MARICOURT	29/7/16	1.30 a.m.	All batteries reopen fire on previous targets.	Ret
		4.15 to 4.55 a.m.	Batteries engaged in bombardment west of GUILLEMONT.	
		4.55 a.m.	Batteries return to wire zones.	
		5 a.m.	All guns of Howitzer Battery on branches of Ravine S.W. of GUILLEMONT.	
		6 p.m.	Section of Hows. turned on to strong point S.W. of GUILLEMONT.	
		10 p.m. onwards	18 pdrs of Group wire cutting. Howitzers on Trench east of ARROW HEAD COPSE.	Ret
	30.7.16	4.45 a.m.	Support attack on GUILLEMONT.	
		6 a.m.	Infantry reach Eastern edge of GUILLEMONT. Held up there.	
		1.25 p.m.	Infantry retiring to Western edge of GUILLEMONT. Artillery barrage follows.	Ret

WAR DIARY or INTELLIGENCE SUMMARY

Army Form C. 2118.

(Erase heading not required.)

Instructions regarding War Diaries and Intelligence Summaries are contained in F. S. Regs., Part II. and the Staff Manual respectively. Title Pages will be prepared in manuscript.

Place	Date	Hour	Summary of Events and Information	Remarks and references to Appendices
NEAR MARICOURT	30/7/16	4 pm onwards	Slow barrage west of GUILLEMONT.	Ref
	31/7/16	1.30 am	Barrage ceases. Batteries (18 pdrs.) on wire zones. Quiet all day. Returned to Adjutant 163rd Brigade R.F.A.	Ref Appendix I. M.O's Summary of Medical & Sanitary work for July. App. II + III Ammunition Expenditure + Casualties since date of Commencement action in XIII Corps area

Appendix I

Summary of Medical and Sanitary work for week ending July 31st 1916

I. **Medical.**
 (a) General health of troops good. No serious prevalent disease.
  (1) Skin trouble, carbuncles, abscess
  (2) Muscular Rheumatism
  (3) Dental
  (4) Other complaints, njuries etc

 (b) No infectious disease.
 (c) Case Conjunctivitis, wounds etc admitted to & & put d

II. **Sanitation**
  All modern types of latrines, urinals in use. Chloride of Lime and Crezol freely employed around kitchens etc Sanitation generally good

D. N. McKenzie
Captain RAMC
SR.

APPENDIX II.

Expenditure of Ammunition since coming into Action in XIII Corps area.
H.S. Howz.

Date	A	AX	B	BX	(Previous Service)
July 21st	1589	214		48	
July 22	1217	289		446	
July 23	1365	439		360	
July 24	1851	451		560	202
July 25	1939	664		277	
July 26	1461	1006		593	
July 27	1913	1432		895	
July 28	1240	644		533	
July 29	2260	483		547	
July 30	1094	622		1076	442
July 31	569	234		901	50

R. Gunner
a/s 103rd Bde RFA

WAR DIARY or INTELLIGENCE SUMMARY

Place	Date	Hour	Summary of Events and Information	Remarks and references to Appendices
			Casualties since date of coming into action in XIII Corps area.	
			July 21st Wounded in Action } 1. Artillery fire. }	
			" 22nd " " 1	
			" 23rd " " 5	
			" 24th " " 2.	
			" 25th " " 1.	
			" 26th " " 1. Killed in action 1.	
			" 27th " " 11	
			" 28th " " 5.	
			" 29th " " nil.	
			" 30th " " 2	
			" 31st nil —	

Returned to A/1.1635 BdeRFA

WAR DIARY

of 163rd (Howitzer) Brigade R.F.A.

This diary runs from

do

to th inclusive.

Drain compiled by du. O.C. & Lt. Ar Symons

163rd BRIGADE

ROYAL FIELD ARTILLERY

AUGUST 1916

35th Divisional Artillery.

vol 7

Cover for Documents.

Nature of Enclosures.

Confidential.
War Diary
of
163rd Brigade R.F.A.
from August 1st — 31st 1916.
Volume 7

Notes, or Letters written.

E J Munro
Lt Col
Comdg 163rd Brigade R.F.A.

WAR DIARY or INTELLIGENCE SUMMARY

Army Form C. 2118.

(Erase heading not required.)

Place	Date	Hour	Summary of Events and Information	Remarks and references to Appendices
Near MARICOURT	1.8.16	8.am.	One section A, B, C, & D Batteries 163, move on relief to positions South of MONTAUBAN. One section of A/151, B/151, C/151, D/150 relieved by sections of 275 Bde. 55th Div. Little firing during the day. Ammunition expended A. ~~376~~ RCT AX. 77 BX. 25 Casualties. Wounded in action O.R. 1. Artillery fire	RCT
Near MONTAUBAN	2.8.16	8.am.	Remaining sections of batteries of 163 Bde move to new positions. Relief of batteries of 151 & 150 Bdes by 275 Bde completed. LT. COL. SYMONDS hands over command of C sub-group to Lt. Col. SHEPPARD, commdg. 275 Bde, & takes over command of sub-group consisting of 4 batteries of 163rd Bde, under Lt. Col. STEWART, Commdg. Group. Group & sub-group attached to 2nd Div. for tactics & discipline. To enable B Battery to rest as many of its personnel as possible, one of its 3 remaining guns with detachments is attached to C Battery, 2 guns to A Battery. One officer of B Battery attached to A & C. Capt. Crocker goes to wagon line.	
		12 noon	Orders for day firing. All batteries to fire on line running from N.W. of GINCHY to W. of GUILLEMONT. Batteries to take one hour in turn. S.O.S. lines allotted running from a point N.N.W. of GUILLEMONT to a point due W. of GUILLEMONT.	
		8.50pm	S.O.S. call received.	
		9.30pm	Halve rate of fire.	Ammunition expended A nil AX nil BX nil
		10pm	Cease firing on SOS lines.	Casualties. Wounded in action O.R. 4 Artillery fire RCT

WAR DIARY or INTELLIGENCE SUMMARY

Army Form C. 2118

(Erase heading not required.)

Place	Date	Hour	Summary of Events and Information	Remarks and references to Appendices
Near MONTAUBAN.	3.8.16	8.50pm	Orders received to stop firing on present barrage lines.	
		10pm	Orders received to fire on area extending about 1000 yards East of GUILLEMONT from a line running about 1000 yards N. from the S.E. edge of Guillemont. Object, to harass the enemy's ration-supply & relief. Half the allowance of ammunition for 18pdrs to be expended between 12 midnight & 4 a.m. C.O. leaves for wagon lines, having sprained his ankle. Ammunition Expended A 351 AX 131 BX 140. Casualties. Wounded 1 O.R. Artillery fire.	RCT
"	4.8.16	7.50pm	Orders received to reduce extent of S.O.S. line by about 400 yards. Position remains the same.	
		9.40pm	S.O.S. call received.	Ammunition Expended. A 601. AX 178 BX 91
		9.50pm	Order to stop firing on S.O.S. lines.	Casualties. Wounded O.R. by Artillery fire. RCT
"	5.8.16	8.30pm	Orders received to increase the allowance of ammunition between hours of 8.30pm and 8.30am. 300 rds per 18pdr battery to be fired between those hours on area above mentioned. 150 rounds by How Bty	
		—	1 gun of A Battery put out of action owing to scoring on inner tube. A Battery now has 2 guns only, one having been handed over to 30th Div. as ordered by 35 DA.	
		9.5pm	S.O.S. call received.	Ammunition expended A 340. AX 73 BX 74.
		9.15pm	Stop firing on S.O.S lines	Casualties. NIL. RCT

WAR DIARY
or
INTELLIGENCE SUMMARY

(Erase heading not required.)

Army Form C. 2118.

Instructions regarding War Diaries and Intelligence Summaries are contained in F.S. Regs., Part II. and the Staff Manual respectively. Title Pages will be prepared in manuscript.

Place	Date	Hour	Summary of Events and Information	Remarks and references to Appendices
Near MONTAUBAN	6.8.16	4 pm	All batteries fire on disused gun emplacement, suspected of being infantry dug outs.	
		4 pm	2nd D.A. Operation Order No 27 received. Copy attached	Appendix I Operation Order 2nd DA No 27
		4 pm	Order received that S.O.S. signal is now 5 red parachute rockets fired in succession.	
		9.35 pm	Orders received that 18 pdrs are to carry out Chinese attack No.3 in conjunction with Heavy Artillery on the 7th	
			Ammunition expended A. 668 AX 82, BX 164.	
			Casualties. Wounded O.R. 1. Artillery fire.	R.T.
	7.8.16	1.55 pm	18 pdr. batteries carry out Chinese attack referred to above.	Appendix II 2nd DA Operation Order No 29
		3 pm	Lt. Col. STEWART sees battery commanders at Bde. H.Q. in connection with 2nd DA Operation orders No.27. & also No.29. copy of which is attached.	
			2/Lt. R.L. MAITLAND-HERIOT detailed to act as Liaison officer at H.Q of 17th MIDDLESEX. Zero time for O.O. No.27 announced as 4.20 am. * X time as 4.0 am.	
		9 pm	Zero time altered to 4.2 am. 18 pdr. batteries to lift 150 yds at Zero minus 15 minutes: at Zero minus 12 minutes return to original line. From Zero onwards, no change.	* ie commencement of barrage

WAR DIARY or INTELLIGENCE SUMMARY

Army Form C. 2118.

(Erase heading not required.)

Place	Date	Hour	Summary of Events and Information	Remarks and references to Appendices
Near MONTAUBAN	7.8.16	9.15 pm	C.O. returns from wagon lines.	
		—	Neighbourhood of battery positions heavily and Bde H.Q. heavily shelled during the night.	
			Ammunition expended A 642. AX 179 BX 154.	
			Casualties. Wounded O.R. 1. Artillery fire.	R.C.T.
	8.8.16	4.2 am	Attack on GUILLEMONT by 2nd + 55th Divs opens. (vide 2nd D.A. Operation Order No. 27.)	
		7.15 am	C Battery reports 1 gun out of action.	
		7.15 am	Group report KINGS + MIDDLESEX have joined up in Z-Z Trench.	
		7.20	Slacken rate of fire to 1 round per gun per 2 minutes.	
		7.50 am	Increase rate of fire to 1 round per gun per minute.	
		9.40 am	C Battery report another gun out of action. Total number of 18 pdrs. now in action 7.	
		12. noon	1 How. reported out of action.	

WAR DIARY
or
INTELLIGENCE SUMMARY
(Erase heading not required.)

Army Form C. 2118.

Instructions regarding War Diaries and Intelligence Summaries are contained in F. S. Regs., Part II. and the Staff Manual respectively. Title Pages will be prepared in manuscript.

Place	Date	Hour	Summary of Events and Information	Remarks and references to Appendices
Near MONTAUBAN.	8.9.16	12.35 pm.	Order received to slacken rate of fire for 18 pdrs. to 1 rd. per gun per 2 mins.	
		12.50 pm.	How. battery reports 4 guns again in action.	
		2.45 pm.	Reduce rate of fire for 18 pdrs to 1 round per gun every 4 minutes.	
		4.0 pm to 5 pm.	1. 18 pdr Battery (A Battery) on whole line T.13.C.4.9. – T.13.d.5.1. (see map)	
		5 pm to 6 pm.	C Battery as above	
		7 pm to 9 pm.	A Battery as above	
		8.17 pm.	S.O.S. call received.	
		8.40 pm.	Stop firing on S.O.S. lines.	
		9.10 pm.	2nd D.A. Operation Order No. 30 received. Attack on GUILLEMONT to be repeated on the 9th. Zero time & lines of barrage remain the same.	
		9.30 pm to 12.30 pm	Howitzer Battery on final barrage area, 6 salvoes an hour.	

WAR DIARY
or
INTELLIGENCE SUMMARY

(Erase heading not required.)

Army Form C. 2118.

Instructions regarding War Diaries and Intelligence Summaries are contained in F. S. Regs., Part II. and the Staff Manual respectively. Title Pages will be prepared in manuscript.

Place	Date	Hour	Summary of Events and Information	Remarks and references to Appendices
Near MONTAUBAN	8.8.16		Ammunition expended. A 2703. AX 1177. BX 1883. Casualties Killed 1 O.R. (Artillery fire). Wounded 1 O.R. (Artillery fire)	RCT
"	9.8.16	2.30am to 3.30 am	All guns on final barrage. 18 pdrs 1 rd p.g. per min. Hows 1 rd p.g. per 2 min	
		3.30am to 4 am	All guns on final barrage. Half above rate of fire.	
		4.10 am	Artillery support attack on GUILLEMONT. vide operation Order No. 30*	*Copy attached Appendix III
		7.45 am	Stop firing	
		8.30 am to 9.30 am	A Battery on line T 13 c 4.9 — T 13 d 5.1 20 salvoes.	
		9.30 to 10.30 am	C Battery as above.	
		9.38 am	Rate of fire reduced to 12 salvoes	

WAR DIARY or INTELLIGENCE SUMMARY

Army Form C. 2118

Place	Date	Hour	Summary of Events and Information	Remarks and references to Appendices
Near MONTAUBAN	9.8.16	10 am	S.O.S. lines altered to T.13d.1.0 – S.24.d.9.9.	
		11.30 am to 12.30 pm	A Battery on duty firing as at 8.30 am. on line T.13.c.4.9 to T.13.d.5.1	Amm expended A.1360. AX 658 BX 992 Casualties wounded OR 4 Artillery fire
		12.30 pm to 1.30 pm	C Battery " " " " 9.30 am	
		5.30 pm to 6.30 pm	A Battery " " firing on same line at same rate (12 salvoes)	
		6.30 pm to 7.30 pm	C Battery " " " " " " " "	
		8.30 pm to 10.30 pm	A Battery " " " " " " " "	
		10.30 pm to 12.30 am	C Battery " " " " " " " "	
"	10.8.16		A Battery on duty 2.30 am to 4.30 am + 8.30 am to 10.30 am + 2.30 pm – 4.30 pm	
			C Battery " " 4.30 am – 6.30 am + 10.30 am to 12.30 am + 4.30 pm – 6.30 pm	

WAR DIARY or INTELLIGENCE SUMMARY

Army Form C.2118.

(Erase heading not required.)

Place	Date	Hour	Summary of Events and Information	Remarks and references to Appendices
Near MONTAUBAN	10.8.16	4.15 pm	Zone & S.O.S. lines changed to area S.W. of GUILLEMONT. (T 25 a 0.7 to T 25 a 0.0.). Night firing both batteries on T 19 b + d + T 25 b 300 rounds per battery to be fired by 18 pdrs between 8.30 pm + 8.am, 150 rounds by Howitzer battery. Ammunition expended A. 572 AX. 14. B nil BX nil. Casualties nil.	RCT
	11.8.16	8.am to 10 am	Relief of 1 section of each battery by 1 section of batteries of 107 Bde, 24th Div. completed.	
		10 am	C Battery report another gun out of action owing to scoring and corrosion of inner tube.	
		10.30 am	Day firing orders received. Batteries (18 pdr) to fire 100 rounds before 8.30 pm on this Brigade Zone. How battery 50 rounds. Ammunition expended A. 501. AX. 133 B. 155. BX 33. Casualties nil.	RCT

WAR DIARY or INTELLIGENCE SUMMARY.

Army Form C. 2118.

(Erase heading not required.)

Hour, Date, Place		Summary of Events and Information	Remarks and references to Appendices
Near MONTAUBAN. 12.8.16.	10 am	Relief of Bde HQ + batteries by 107 Bde, 24th Div. completed. Ammunition expended, nil. Casualties, nil. Brigade moves to wagon line at GROVETOWN. BRAY.	Ret
13.8.16. GROVETOWN BRAY	10.45 am 11.30 am	Bde moves to new camp BOIS DES TAILLES NORTH arrives new camp. CRA visits camp in afternoon.	Ret
14.8.16. BOIS DES TAILLES NORTH	8 am 5.30 pm	Orders received that Bde will move to VILLE SUR ANCRE in evening. Bde moves to VILLE-SUR-ANCRE.	
VILLE-SUR-ANCRE.	7.30 pm	arrives new camp.	Ret
15.8.16.	11 am "	G.O.C. 35th Division inspects Bde. Orders received that Bde is to reinforce 3rd D.A. on the 16th	

Hour, Date, Place	Summary of Events and Information	Remarks and references to Appendices
VILLE-SUR-ANCRE. 15.8.16 12.30 pm	C.O. and battery commanders visit 3rd D.A. and reconnoitre new positions.	
VILLE-SUR-ANCRE 16.8.16 9.30 am	Bde moves to line. Wagon lines at GROVE TOWN, BRAY. Battery positions in orchard east of MARICOURT. Bde H.Q. in Trenches west of MARICOURT.	Ret
MARICOURT. 7 pm to 8 pm	Guns brought into position. [11 18pdrs 4 Hows. Guns required to replace guns defective or with I.O.M. obtained from 159 & 157 Bdes in accordance with 35 D.A.'s instructions. B Battery comes into action with 3 guns only.]	Ret
" 17.8.16	Batteries registering. Zone allotted from right hand edge of WEDGE WOOD to left hand edge of OAKHANGER WOOD	

WAR DIARY or INTELLIGENCE SUMMARY

Army Form C. 2118.

Hour, Date, Place	Summary of Events and Information	Remarks and references to Appendices
MARICOURT. 17.8.16 cont'd	Ammunition expended A 61. AX 29 B nil BX 33 Casualties nil	
18.8.16. 8 am	Operation Order received. 3rd Division in conjunction with the 24th Division on its left, & the French 153rd Division on its right to attack German Trench system between GUILLEMONT and ANGLE WOOD, exclusive, on the 18th and 19th. Task of 163rd Bde to fire on valley running from behind WEDGE WOOD in a north & then N.E. direction: also on about 500-600 yards of trenches running from N. end of WEDGE WOOD towards S.E. corner of GUILLEMONT: also to sweep the crest running N & S. in front of WEDGE WOOD.	
2.45 pm	Zero time.	
4.45 pm	Infantry to reach 2nd objective.	

WAR DIARY or INTELLIGENCE SUMMARY.

Army Form C. 2118.

Hour, Date, Place	Summary of Events and Information	Remarks and references to Appendices
MARICOURT. 18.8.16. 6.10pm	Orders received to sweep road WEDGEWOOD - GUILLEMONT.	
6.30pm	Orders received to search & sweep line from LEUZE WOOD to WEDGE WOOD. Germans reported advancing in this direction	
7.20pm	Batteries ordered to return to original targets.	
7.45pm	Stop firing.	
	C.O. at OLD WOOD O.P. during above operations	
9.30pm	NIGHT LINES allotted, on line in front of trenches WEDGEWOOD - FALFEMONT. Hows. on valley behind WEDGE WOOD. Ammunition expended A 1496 AX 587 B nil BX 719 Casualties nil.	Ret
19.8.16 12.5.am	Orders received that 3rd and 4th phases of above operations which were to have taken place at 5 am and 6 am respectively are cancelled.	
10.am	1 18pdr battery & Hows. on valley behind WEDGE WOOD, occasional salvos. 2 other 18pdr. batteries on line in front of WEDGE WOOD - FALFEMONT. Stop firing 8.30pm.	Amm. expended A 180 AX 11 BX 57 Casualties nil Ret

WAR DIARY
or
INTELLIGENCE SUMMARY.
(Erase heading not required.)

Army Form C. 2118.

Instructions regarding War Diaries and Intelligence Summaries are contained in F.S. Regs., Part II. and the Staff Manual respectively. Title pages will be prepared in manuscript.

Hour, Date, Place	Summary of Events and Information	Remarks and references to Appendices
MARICOURT. 20.8.16. 10.50 a.m.	All guns onto line T 25 d 2 8 – B 16 8 9 : search north eastwards.	
8.10 p.m.	Stop firing. C.O. with C.R.A. 35th Div. to HARDECOURT. Ammunition expended A 453. AX 73 BX 145 Casualties nil	Ret
21.8.16. 7 a.m.	18 pdrs. on line B.16.8.6 to T.25.d.3.9. searching NE up valley Hows. on valley behind WEDGE WOOD	
8.20 p.m.	Stop firing Ammunition expended. A 575 AX 144 BX 290. Casualties nil.	Ret
22.8.16	All guns & hows. on same targets. from 6 a.m. to 8.10 p.m. Ammunition expended. A 603 AX 105 BX 357 Casualties wounded O.R. 1. (Artillery fire)	Ret

WAR DIARY or INTELLIGENCE SUMMARY

Army Form C. 2118.

Hour, Date, Place	Summary of Events and Information	Remarks and references to Appendices
MARICOURT. 23.8.16	6 am. All guns reopen fire on same targets. 8.15 pm. Stop firing. Ammunition expended. A 857 AX 81 BX 858 Casualties. Nil.	Pct
24.8.16	1.30 am Operation Order received for attack to be made by Fourth Army in conjunction with the French on our right. XIV Corps to attack both N. & S. of GUILLEMONT, 35th Division on the right, 20th Division on the left. Howitzers of 163 Bde to fire on line T.25.b.3.2. to T.25.d.7.9½. From Zero minus 2 hours. 18 pdrs on valley behind WEDGEWOOD. 2.30 pm. Order received that infantry attack by 35th Division is cancelled. Infantry only to advance their right with the French. Artillery programme modified.	

WAR DIARY or INTELLIGENCE SUMMARY.

Army Form C. 2118.

Hour, Date, Place	Summary of Events and Information	Remarks and references to Appendices
MARICOURT. 24.8.16. (Cont'd)	2 batteries of 18 pdrs on line B.1.b.7.6 - B.2.a.50 from Zero onwards. 1 battery searching back from that line along the Eastern slope of WEDGE WOOD valley from Zero onwards. Howitzers to remain on Target already given.	
	C.O. and Capt. Goss go to O.P. near HARDECOURT to observe.	
5.45 pm	Zero time for above operation.	
5.45 pm	F.O.O. reports that FRENCH have left their trenches N. of MAUREPAS.	
5.50 pm	F.O.O. reports small parties of Germans are coming out of their Trenches and surrendering.	
5.51 pm	F.O.O. reports British deploying from line B.2.a.0.2 to B.2.c.6.1	
6.0 pm	F.O.O. reports British digging in on above line.	

Hour, Date, Place	Summary of Events and Information	Remarks and references to Appendices
MARICOURT 24.8.16	All above and subsequent messages from F.O.O. transmitted to CRA 3rd Division as soon as received.	
6.7 pm	Order received from CRA to move barrage ~~northwards~~ on GUILLEMONT – FALFEMONT line ~~northwards~~ let so as not to interfere with our infantry in view of F.O.O's 6 pm message ~~................~~ let. A battery ordered to fire on line B2a3.8 – B2a7.5½ B " " " " " " T26c0.4 – B2a8.8 C " " " " Lift 300 yards & sweep N.E.	
6.12 pm	F.O.O. reports FRENCH in force in trench running from B2d7.3 – B8a2.0 Some of them 500 yards in front of this. Our infantry do not appear able to get forward. They are still digging in on same line.	
6.24 pm	F.O.O reports Our infantry have got forward a little. Casualties heavy. FRENCH are fighting in OAKHANGER. Several parties	

WAR DIARY or INTELLIGENCE SUMMARY.

(Erase heading not required.)

Army Form C. 2118.

Hour, Date, Place	Summary of Events and Information	Remarks and references to Appendices
MARICOURT. 24.8.16.	of the enemy surrendering there	
6.48 pm	FRENCH have pushed forward along road as far as B3d 5.6. (F.O.O.'s report)	
6.52 pm	F.O.O. reports ammunition has just gone forward to our infantry who do not appear to be much in advance of a line from B2c 9.4 to B2c 5.8 & there are none of them to the N. of the latter point. They are not in any strength but appear to be well dug in.	
7.0 pm	Order received from C.R.A. not to fire south of a line running E & W through middle of WEDGE WOOD. Search valley behind WEDGEWOOD. Part of FALFEMONT thought to be held by us. A & C Batteries ordered to search & sweep valley behind WEDGEWOOD. B. to fire on line T26c 0.4½ to T25d 8.8½. None to fire south of line above mentioned.	
7.5 pm	F.O.O. reports small parties of our infantry appear to be in or close up to GERMAN Trench B2d 5.5. They are being heavily shelled.	

WAR DIARY
or
INTELLIGENCE SUMMARY.
(Erase heading not required.)

Army Form C. 2118.

Hour, Date, Place	Summary of Events and Information	Remarks and references to Appendices

MARICOURT 24.8.16.	7.11 pm. Heavy GERMAN barrage reported by F.O.O. in front of FALFEMONT.
	
	 7.20 pm. Orders received from C.R.A. to bring barrage down to FALFEMONT, not firing south of B.2.a. central; as report has been received that we do not hold FALFEMONT.
	
	    A Battery ordered to fire on line B.2.a central to
	            T 26 C 0 7.
	
	    C Battery " " T 26 C 2.0. to
	            T 25 d 9.4½
	
	    B Battery to remain on present line. All batteries to search 200 – 1000 yards N.E.
	
	 7.37 pm. F.O.O. reports no red lights seen from infantry at 7.30 pm as indicated in operation order.	

WAR DIARY
or
INTELLIGENCE SUMMARY.

(Erase heading not required.)

Army Form C. 2118.

Instructions regarding War Diaries and Intelligence Summaries are contained in F.S. Regs., Part II. and the Staff Manual respectively. Title pages will be prepared in manuscript.

Hour, Date, Place	Summary of Events and Information	Remarks and references to Appendices
MARICOURT. 24.8.16		
8 pm	F.O.O. reports 2 red lights just seen from FALFEMONT. Wounded report that a company of infantry is in FALFEMONT. 2 red lights seen from OAKHANGER about B.3.c.5.4.	
9.50 pm	Orders received from C.R.A. not to fire south of a line running E & W. through T.26.c.2.2. C Battery ordered not to fire S. of above point and to barrage from there to T.25.d.9.6., searching occasionally N.E.	
10.30 pm	Order received to stop firing.	
	Ammunition expended. A.798 AX.258 BX.618 Casualties nil	
25.8.16 10.15 am	Orders received to fire on square T.25.d T.26.c+d. A Battery ordered to sweep T.26.d not firing South of a line running E & W through S. end of WEDGEWOOD	

WAR DIARY or INTELLIGENCE SUMMARY.

Army Form C. 2118.

(Erase heading not required.)

Hour, Date, Place	Summary of Events and Information	Remarks and references to Appendices
MARICOURT. 25.8.16 (contd).	Orders received that the Brigade is to go out of action to-day, 25th.	
12.40 pm		
7.0 pm	Orders received to stop firing.	
9.0 pm	A Battery pulls out.	
9.30 pm	B " "	
10.0 pm	C " "	
10.30 pm	D " "	
	8, 18 pdrs handed over to 3rd D.A. Brigade takes with it on going out of action 2. 18 pdrs 3 Hows. 2. 18 pdrs & 1 How being with I.O.M	
	Ammunition expended. A 849. AX 463 BX 633. Casualties nil	

Ret

WAR DIARY or INTELLIGENCE SUMMARY.

Army Form C. 2118.

Hour, Date, Place	Summary of Events and Information	Remarks and references to Appendices
BOIS DES TAILLES NORTH. 26.8.16 10.30am.	Brigade H.Q. moves to BOIS DES TAILLES NORTH.	
2.30pm	Batteries move to BOIS DES TAILLES NORTH marching off in order, A, B, C, D, at half-hourly intervals.	Ref
27.8.16	C.O. Adjutant, Capt. GOSS, Lt. MORGAN, proceed on 3 days leave to PARIS.	Ref
28.8.16	Nothing to record.	Ref
29.8.16	Nothing to record.	Ref
30.8.16	C.O. Adjt. Capt Goss and Lt MORGAN return from leave	Ref
31.8.16	Nothing to record.	Ref Appendix IV M.O.'s Summary of Medical Sanitary work for July.

Returned Lt.
O/c. 163rd Brigade RFA

D/59 + Sub Franks.

Barrage before ZERO will be amended as follows :-

ALL BATTERIES   Barrage commenced at
ZERO minus 18 mins.

ALL 18 pdr Batteries D/36 + 56th 13/y
At ZERO minus 15 min. left 150 yds.
At ZERO minus 12' min return to original
zero.
From ZERO onwards, no change.

7/8/16

ZAPPA
AY EXPEDE

S. Z. Ford
2.7 July
Rly Manifogmane
Whilehaven fair + your
Buttermere.
The area for this list is
very small, & in the first parts
(B) + (C), all the Butternute
fue on the same sheet.

Ia (C) rt 28 Septem 20, the
line edible chanted, Betemeny 1638 10th
they fm 7/30/4 9 & 7/3 d 24, t
the 1078th (Chithamer rly of quin)
fm 7/3 d 24 — 7/3 d 5/1.

J.J. Havard
NCC
Ephale
5/9/16

2nd Divisional Artillery Operation Order No.27

8th August 1916.

Appendix I

1. At a date and hour to be notified later 2nd and 55th Divisions will attack and capture GUILLEMONT and the works between it and WATRELOT FARM, also the trench running parallel to the LONGUEVAL - GUILLEMONT road through S 18 d and T 19 a. This trench is known as Z-Z.

2. The first objective of 2nd Division is the northern part of Z-Z and the front line trench from S 24 b 5.5 to S 24 d 8.5.
   Later objectives are :-
   At zero plus 10 Machine gun house S 24 b 7.4 and the Station.
   At zero plus 20 line of LONGUEVAL - GUILLEMONT road.
   At zero plus 30 remainder of Z-Z.

3. BARRAGES. Zero is the hour of attack, barrage will commence at a time before zero, to be notified later, this time is called X.

   RATES OF FIRE EXCEPT : 18-prs. 3 rounds per gun per minute.
   WHEN OTHERWISE ORDERED. : 4.5" Hows. 2 rounds per gun per minute.

   34th Brigade - 2 18-pr Batteries.
   From X to zero plus 1 minute.
   Z-Z trench from S 18 d 6.6 to T 19 a 1.6.
   At zero plus 1 minute lift 150 yards and search back 300 yards with shrapnel.

   36th Brigade - 3 18-pr Batteries.
   From X to zero plus 30 minutes.
   Z-Z trench from T 19 a 1.6 to its junction with BROMPTON ROAD at T 19 a 4.0.
   At zero plus 30 minutes lift to line T 13 c 4.0 - T 19 a 8.2 searching back 300 yards with shrapnel.
   At zero plus 40 minutes close in right end of barrage to line T 19 a 6.8 to T 19 b 2.6.

   41st Brigade - 3 18-pr Batteries.
   From X to zero.
   German front line from S 24 b 5.3½ to S 24 d 8.5.
   At zero lift to line T 13 c 8.5 to T 19 d 8.2 searching back 300 yds with shrapnel.
   At zero plus 40 lift to line of trench T 13 c 8.5 to T 19 b 4.4 still searching 300 yards.

   157th and 163rd Brigades - 18-pounders.

   (a) 4.5" Howitzers.   56th Battery.   From X to Zero plus 1.
       Area enclosed by S 24 b 7.0 - T 19 a 4.2 - T 19 a 4.0 - T 19 c 0.7½.
   (b) At Zero plus 10, lift 150 yards.
   (c) At Zero plus 20, lift to line of trench T 13 c 4.9 to T 13 d 5.1 searching back 300 yards.

   D/36th Battery.   From X to Zero plus 30 minutes.
   Z-Z trench from T 19 a 1.6 to T 19 a 4.0. then lift.
   Z-Z trench from T 19 a 1.6 then lift to road T 13 a 1.0 to T 13 a 9.0.

P. T. B.

4.5"Howitzers (continued).

47th Battery. From X to Zero plus 30 minutes.
Trench along BROMPTON ROAD T 19 a 4.0 to T 19 a 5½.½

D/157 Battery. X to Zero plus 20 minutes.
Trench along BROMPTON ROAD from Cross roads at T 19 c 2½.8½ to T 19 a 4.0 then lift.

D/163 Battery. X to Zero plus 10.
Machine gun house S 24 b 7.4 and trench from there to railway at S 24 b 9¾.½ then lift.

All howitzer batteries, except 56th when lifted will search areas north and east of GINCHY as follows:-

D/36 Battery. T 14 a.
47th   "   T 14 c.
D/157   "   T 20 a.
D/163   "   T 13 b.

At zero plus 40 minutes Howitzers will drop to 1 round per gun per minute.
At zero plus 70 minutes 18-pounders will drop to 1 round per gun per minute.
All barrage lines must be registered with great care, To-day and to-morrow August 6th and 7th will be available for this purpose.

ACKNOWLEDGE.

Carrington
Major R.A.
Brigade Major R.A. 2nd Division.

2nd Divisional Artillery Operation Order No.29.

7th August 1916.

The following communications will be established for the attack on GUILLEMONT:-

Colonel Stewart 35th D.A. will be at 6th Inf.Bde.H.Q. and establish communication from there to his own Group.
BERNAFAY Station will be manned by Colonel Newcombe, and 1 Officer 36th Bde., 1 Officer 34th Bde.

The 34th Bde. 1 Officer and party will establish a station in TRONES WOOD.

36th Bde. and Explode Group will each provide an officer and party at WATERLOT FARM.

36th Bde. will be in touch with 1st/Kings.
Explode Group to 17th/Middlesex, whose H.Q. are close to the abovenamed place.

The 41st Bde. will establish a station in the neighbourhood of ARROW HEAD COPSE.

The above out-stations will arrange their own communication with the BERNAFAY Station, having receiving parties at BERNAFAY as well. Venetian shutters and French lamps ought to prove useful auxiliaries.

The origin of a message is most important it should be stated whether the event reported was seen personally or hearsay. Time of event is essential.

R. Carrie Moon
Major R.A.
Brigade Major R.A. 2nd Divn.

SECRET   Appendix III

2nd Divisional Artillery Operation
Order No 30
8th Aug. 1916

1. This morning's operation will be
repeated tomorrow.

2. Zero hour will be the same as to-day.

3. All Batteries open fire at 4.10 a.m. on
line of final barrage to-day and so
continue till further orders.
Rate of fire
    4.10 am to 5.30 am
    18 pdr. 3 rounds per gun per minute
    4.5" How. 2 rounds per gun per minute
    5.30 am onwards
    18 pdr. 1½ rds. 4.5" How.
    1 rd. per gun per minute

8.8.16.

Appendix IV

MEDICAL & SANITARY REPORT
of 163rd Bde R.F.A., for month ending 31st Aug 1916.

MEDICAL

1. General health of troops good.
2. All ordinary cases treated with unit. Severe injuries, wounds, chronic skin troubles — sent to hospital, as usual.
3. Infectious Disease - Two cases were sent to hospital with suspected Dysentery — one of these had come from another unit, and was diagnosed of the Flexner type. For 3 weeks an abnormal number of diarrhoea cases occurred, but these have now become normal.

SANITARY

1. Sanitation good generally.
2. Ordinary fly-proof latrines in use — with liberal use of chloride of lime, & cresol solution etc.
3. Meat-safes, & food protected by muslin from flies so far as possible.
4. Water-supplies regulated & sufficiently chlorinated.

A.E. Mackenzie
Capt R.A.M.C. (T.R.)

WAR DIARY *or* **INTELLIGENCE SUMMARY**

(Erase heading not required.)

Army Form C. 2118

Instructions regarding War Diaries and Intelligence Summaries are contained in F.S. Regs., Part II. and the Staff Manual respectively. Title Pages will be prepared in manuscript.

Place	Date	Hour	Summary of Events and Information	Remarks and references to Appendices
BOIS DES TAILLES	1.9.16	—	Nothing to record.	Ret
"	2.9.16	—	Brigade receives guns from 3rd D.A. to replace guns lent on the 26th August. Brigade now has its full number of guns.	Ret
DAOURS	3.9.16	8.30 am	Brigade moves to DAOURS, arriving about 1 pm.	Ret
MOLLIENS AU-BOIS	4.9.16	1.45 pm	Brigade moves to MOLLIENS-AU-BOIS marching via ALLONVILLE and RAINNEVILLE. Arrives 5 pm.	Ret
MONPLAISIR	5.9.16	10. am.	Brigade moves to area MONPLAISIR - OCCOCHES - LE QUESNEL. A Battery billetted at LEQUESNES, B Battery and Bde H.Q. at MONPLAISIR, C Battery and D Battery at OCCOCHES.	Ret
MEZEROLLES	6.9.16	1.30 pm	Brigade moves to MEZEROLLES, arriving 3.0. pm.	Ret
	7.9.16	8. am	Orders received re reorganization of Divisional Artillery. A Battery is to be absorbed into 157 Bde, B Battery and D Battery	

WAR DIARY
~~INTELLIGENCE SUMMARY~~
(Erase heading not required.)

Army Form C. 2118.

Place	Date	Hour	Summary of Events and Information	Remarks and references to Appendices
B2 BROLLES	7.9.16	—	into 158 Bde, C Battery into 159 Bde. Capt. CROCKER to Command B/158, Capt. SANDERSON to command C/158, Capt. KEITH to command A/157. Reorganization to take effect from 8.a.m. 8/9/16. Lt. Col. SYMONDS to command 35 D.A. Details Ret	
"	—	2.15 p.m.	Brigade moves to LE SOUICH. B, C, and D Batteries join their new Brigades, leaving 2/Lts HARPER BROOK, and POLFORD with Details	
"	8.9.16	7. a.m.	A Battery joins 157 Bde. leaving Lt HOLDER, and 2/Lts FERGUSON and TAGGART with Details	
	—	8. a.m.	163 Bde ceases to exist.	

Returns to.
as/b. 163 Bde RFA.